AMR MUNEER DAHAB

authorHOUSE°

AuthorHouse™
1663 Liberty Drive
Bloomington, IN 47403
www.authorhouse.com
Phone: 833-262-8899

Published by AuthorHouse 11/10/2021

ISBN: 978-1-6655-4422-1 (sc)
ISBN: 978-1-6655-4431-3 (e)

To everyone who has inspired me and to everyone I might have inspired, regardless of the manner or extent of the inspiration.

CONTENTS

PREFACE

Inspiration is not limited to writers, artists, and creators. Inspiration is within everyone's reach.

We all draw inspiration and inspire others, even if we don't realize it.

This book will help you to value inspiration as a necessary and useful process for your life, and to recognize the influence of the inspiration that affects you spontaneously (and you do not notice it directly) and the inspiration you should strive for.

INSPIRATION, NOT IMITATION

1

- ☼ Imitation is almost a mechanical process. Inspiration is creativity that includes a deep spiritual dimension.

- ☼ Imitation is like making a copy of a paper without understanding its content. Inspiration is like reading a paper, absorbing its content, and thinking about how you can benefit from it.

- ☼ Slow down a bit before you start imitating. You can get more useful and sustainable results when you think about how you can tailor any outcome to your own inclination and objectives.

- ☼ In the long run, literal imitation and deep inspiration often have opposite outcomes.

- ☼ If you hasten to literal imitation and adopt a behavior or action without careful thought, nothing should prevent you from rethinking your choice and seeing how you can deeply draw inspiration from the original idea you imitated. Inspiration is not a rare opportunity that vanishes if you wait too long. There is always a chance to correct what you have imitated and turn it into rich inspiration.

- If someone puts forth an idea that you had intended to adopt and promote, do not despair. There are many ideas you can create and develop. You can still work on presenting that same idea, as long as your innovations are genuine.

- If someone buys an item in a new trend that you really like, make sure you genuinely need it before you buy it too. If you are confident that you need that item, find an opportunity to change your choice in some way, instead of buying exactly the same item.

- Do not be upset if you occasionally imitate someone else's behavior or actions. Imitation is a concern only when it becomes habitual.

- The difference between literal imitation and inspiration is that imitation makes you feel satisfied once you have completed it, while inspiration gives you a strong incentive to carry on in some way.

☀ Don't get annoyed when someone imitates you. Their imitation may mean that you were a source of deep inspiration, but your imitator did not know how to be inspired by you as they should have been.

FIELDS OF INSPIRATION

2

- When you believe in the significance of inspiration, inspiration will affect all areas of your life.

- There is no field in which it is difficult to draw inspiration. The doors of inspiration open before you in any field, as long as you love it and are eager to explore the sources of inspiration within it.

- Inspiration is proportional to the intensity of the desire for creativity, regardless of the field.

- No field or act is entirely devoid of inspiration. Even literal imitation can be considered as the slightest degree of inspiration.

- You are most inspiring and most ready to receive inspiration in the field you love most.

- Don't limit your search for inspiration to your field; expand it by looking in all fields. This will multiply your chances of getting the inspiration you seek within your field.

- If sources of inspiration outside your field inspire you to seek a practical or intellectual path parallel to your field or even to change to an entirely new field, don't hesitate. Life is constantly open for you to choose what suits you, and you are never too old to decide to enter a new field. You just need deep, careful thought to make the decision that you see fit.

- In all fields, even those best known for inspiration, people differ in their appreciation of inspiration and their responses to it. Whatever your field, give inspiration as much value as you can to get the best value from it.

- Don't despair if people in your field don't pay enough attention to the value of inspiration. On the contrary, use this as motivation for you to be a pioneer among those around you to emphasize the significance of inspiration.

- The challenges of inspiration are not always confined to purely practical fields; they are found even in the fields best known for inspiration, such as the arts and literature. Deal with these challenges with patience and love in order to enjoy the field itself and seize the creativity to which you aspire.

WHO CAN INSPIRE YOU?

3

- 💡 Any human being—indeed, any being whatsoever—can inspire you.

- 💡 You are the only one who puts limits on the list of those who can inspire you.

- 💡 The person who inspires you is not necessarily better than you. In inspiration, all that matters is the deep benefit and reflection of the inspiration, regardless of the nature of the inspiration and who inspired whom.

- 💡 "Who inspired whom?" is a question that is open to all possibilities. Even during a course on inspiration, participants can be a rich source of inspiration for the coach if the coach is open-minded.

- 💡 Someone who inspires you doesn't tell you that they are going to inspire you so that you can get ready. You will be drawn to those who inspire you with all your senses.

- Admiration fades as you get accustomed to a person, no matter how great or rare their talents are. Do not let your familiarity with those around you block the sources of inspiration in them.

- Animals always have been a source of deep inspiration to humans, inspiring humanity to fly, dive, and master many abstract skills. Do not disdain being inspired by creatures that depend on their basic instincts for survival.

- Others will inspire you with what you don't have, as well as with what you do have and need to develop, whether or not you're aware of what you need. Just keep your heart and mind unreservedly open to inspiration.

- As you read the stories of successful people for inspiration, you will come across secondary characters with special skills and achievements of their own. Don't hesitate to notice these characters and reflect on how they can inspire you.

- You are one of the most important sources of your own inspiration. Look at your past, near and distant, and consider how you behaved in previous situations. Your best source of inspiration is that which you have in your hands.

WHOM SHOULD YOU INSPIRE?

- You are an inspiration to someone. Let this fact increase your confidence and make you more inspiring for others.

- Inspiration is not a task that you perform, but keep in mind that you will inspire many people in one way or another. This fact should give you a lot of confidence and poise.

- While you are busy teaching and guiding some people, you will inspire many others without addressing them directly. You don't choose the people you inspire; they choose you. Often, the inspiration process is spontaneous, without the intention of either party.

- While your measured actions and calm demeanor will inspire some persons, your tough stance, when required, will be equally inspiring to others.

- When engaged in a battle of any kind, your smart and solid stances will inspire your opponents. This is a service you offer involuntarily to those opponents, but you should be proud of that anyway.

- When you are a role model for someone, that person is constantly ready to receive inspiration from you. It is wise to be careful in your behavior for their sake, but don't be fake or pretentious, or you will lose your ability to inspire in the long run.

- You cannot inspire anyone in everything. Accordingly, those you inspire in a particular field may themselves be a source of inspiration for you in other fields. Sometimes, those you inspire may give you inspiration flashes in the same field.

- Although it may seem unfortunate, you may inspire those who are distant from you more than those who are close to you.

- If you teach in any field, your work will be complete when you communicate information to your students so they understand it and pass the exam. Inspiration requires you to pay attention to what will remain in the minds of your students for the rest of their lives.

RICH SOURCES OF INSPIRATION

5

- ☼ Those who are close to you and with whom you deal constantly are often the source of your renewed inspiration. Whoever loves you gives you the greatest gifts of inspiration.

- ☼ Classic and modern means of acquiring knowledge are rich sources of inspiration, some of them particularly so. Books, as a means of knowledge, are unique because they form your inspiration slowly and give you the opportunity to question and argue before your inspiration is fully formed.

- ☼ Your personal experiences may not be your main source of inspiration, but they are certainly the most reliable and sustainable sources of inspiration.

- ☼ New and challenging experiences are highly beneficial. Do not limit your thinking when taking on a new experience full of challenges to how to pass that experience; rather, think about how to be inspired by it.

- Great love is a source of great inspiration, but there is a major difference between being submissive to one's beloved and being inspired by them.

- Certain places and special times often provide inspiration. Take advantage of those places and times to seize inspiration and create opportunities to go to those places devoting yourself to seizing the blessings of inspiration.

- The main objective of a vacation is relaxation, and relaxation stimulates inspiration. Extract from your vacation the maximum sources of inspiration, not as a task you want to finish but as a positive energy that revives your life on a social and professional level.

- The importance and richness of your sources of inspiration change with many factors, most notably age. Renew your sources of inspiration according to changes in yourself at any level. Use a proactive manner; do not wait until the inspiration you are accustomed to dries up before you look for alternatives.

- Do not be alarmed if certain sources of inspiration do not excite anything within you. You can't force inspiration necessarily from certain known sources, and what inspires others might not inspire you. Look for your own sources and expand their circles. It's OK to benefit from the experiences of others without their sources of inspiration becoming an obsession for you.

☀️ While you are busy drawing inspiration from your regular rich sources, don't forget to dig deep for more richness in the sources that seem less rich to you. Use the inspiration itself to enrich the sources of inspiration.

6

SPONTANEOUS INSPIRATION VERSUS IMPOSED INSPIRATION

- ☀ Inspiration is generally considered spontaneous. Spontaneous inspiration is probably the most valuable form of inspiration, but other forms are worthy of appreciation and should be considered for practicing their acquisition skills.

- ☀ There are multiple and graded levels of inspiration, starting from the smooth, spontaneous inspiration to extracting inspiration from seemingly impossible moments. It is good not to give in to the ease of spontaneous inspiration and be satisfied with that. Practice and get used to drawing inspiration within various moments when it does not seem smooth at any level.

- ☀ Spontaneous inspiration is a blessing that you should receive enthusiastically and you shouldn't be distracted by anything else that you can postpone. Immerse yourself in spontaneous inspiration as soon as you feel it knocking on your mind, and stay engrossed until the last drop of inspiration. If you are already preoccupied with something, try to postpone what is left of it, and take time out to receive inspiration and devote yourself to it.

- 💡 Don't immediately take a break when you find inspiration too hard. First try to change the way you think about the subject, or change your place by moving a little to another suitable place. If inspiration remains stubborn, then you can take a break, but be careful not to stray too far from the subject.

- 💡 A period of rest to regain inspiration sometimes becomes an inescapable necessity. This period should not be long, but its duration depends entirely on the nature and stage of the work or the idea that you are processing. It also depends on your mental and psychological state at that time, as well as the time available to complete the work or present the idea in its final form.

- 💡 Set a maximum in advance for a rest period to recover your inspiration; after that maximum, push yourself to continue the work, even if the inspiration still seems difficult. Staying on the lookout for inspiration without a deadline may lead you to quit work altogether or may lead to a noticeable sluggishness and decline in production in the long run.

💡 Inspiration is not thinking, although any thinking process involves some form of inspiration. Talking about stimulating inspiration and working on it means talking about the best ways to allow inspiration to cross into your mind and soul for a richer, broader view of a certain topic, rather than just trying to figure out how to solve an existing or expected problem.

💡 With practice and perseverance and by believing in the importance and value of inspiration, it will become a habit, practiced on every level with interest and passion.

💡 No matter how magical or mysterious the spontaneous inspiration may seem, a deep reflection on the circumstances surrounding the manifestations of your spontaneous inspiration will help you to attract inspiration when you need it and deliberately seek it at any level.

💡 Having a positive attitude will greatly enhance the chances of receiving inspiration.

PRACTICAL INSPIRATION AND EMOTIONAL INSPIRATION

7

- ☀ The nature of inspiration is probably similar in all fields, regardless of whether some are known to be associated with inspiration more than others. Inspiration is more closely related to the nature of the person than to the subject matter of the inspiration.

- ☀ Emotion is deeply involved even in practical inspiration, at least with regard to the great passion that is essential to obtaining deep inspiration, whether purely scientific or practical.

- ☀ When philosophers see the depth of the rhetorical images and meanings that flow from poetry, they wonder how genius found its way to that inspired poet! With that in mind, which one is wronged: genius or inspiration?

- ☀ When people admire a poem, they will probably be amazed at the inspiration that helped the poet to create that particular work. When people admire the work of a scientist, they will probably be amazed at the genius that allowed the scientist to produce that output. With that in mind, which one is wronged: the poet or the scientist?

- Just as artists and writers owe inspiration when producing their masterpieces of creativity, inspiration owes them because, more than scientists and philosophers, it is artists and writers who exalt the value of inspiration and give it its unique charm.

- The job description of artists and writers is not based on inspiration; rather, their masterpieces of creativity are free from the restrictions of any job description.

- The masterpieces of creativity of scholars and thinkers are among the blessings of inspiration as well, but they know how to deal with inspiration while complying with a job description. They may not feel the inspiration directly, or they may call it by another term more appropriate to the nature of their work.

- *Genius* seems to be synonymous with inspiration connected to the mind, apart from the magic of the soul with which inspiration seems more closely connected.

- 🔆 Talented scholars and thinkers in the arts or literature are thought to have the deepest understanding of the difference between genius and inspiration. Their artistic and literary output, however, is not necessarily the highest that embodies the creative fusion of genius and inspiration. Producing unique masterpieces of creativity does not necessarily require accurate knowledge of the details of the concept of genius and the mechanism of inspiration.

- 🔆 The genuinely inspired person does not care to be called a genius.

INDIVIDUAL INSPIRATION AND COLLECTIVE INSPIRATION

8

- ⚬ Within the framework of the collective inspiration in any group, the group members must be prepared to perform as a team before seeing how they deal with inspiration.

- ⚬ Collective inspiration requires great harmony among the members of the group, and its greatest form is that which embodies an entire people.

- ⚬ Collective inspiration is not like a jigsaw puzzle, for which everyone contributes a piece to complete the picture. Rather, it is an interaction through which each idea provokes another idea, leading to the optimal image of inspiration in the desired subject.

- ⚬ Those who are adept at collective inspiration are not necessarily adept at individual inspiration, and vice versa.

- ⚬ It is possible to transfer learning skills from individual inspiration to group inspiration and vice versa, and it is possible for those who are not accustomed to using inspiration skills to learn them. The result, however, depends on the innate readiness of the person and then on how this readiness is discovered and promoted for its development.

- In collective inspiration, one person leads the organization of ideas and the conclusion to the end result. This person is not necessarily the most prolific or the best at inspiration but rather has the most outstanding leadership skills.

- Collective inspiration does not necessarily require participants to be together in one place or even familiar with each other. Ideas that are transmitted through reading or other means of receiving knowledge—among different people in different places and perhaps at different times— are some of the most prominent manifestations of collective inspiration.

- Theft is very likely to occur during collective inspiration, but genuine inspirers are not disturbed by someone stealing one of their ideas. Rather, they continue to inspire with patience, confidence, and love.

- Unless the goal of a member of any collective inspiration team is opposition for the sake of opposition to frustrate creative action, constructive disagreement is one of the best catalysts for inspirational ideas.

💡 The interaction of humans in building human civilization throughout history seems to be the most wonderful embodiment of the concept of collective inspiration.

INSPIRATION THROUGH REJECTION

9

- ☀ Inspiration does not necessarily mean admiration. When someone inspires you, it means that they have had a profound impact on you in some way, regardless of whether you like that person or not.

- ☀ Actions and reactions that you greatly admire or that provoke you most are often your source of inspiration, regardless of your position on who did them.

- ☀ The rejection of an idea or topic, whether from you or another, is inspiring when it is strong and has clear reasons. A weak rejection arouses pity, not inspiration.

- ☀ Do not let the strong rejection in any situation destroy you or cause you any grief. Rather, look for an opportunity for inspiration within that rejection, whether with regard to the subject of rejection or to taking positions in general.

- The strong *no* usually has a lot behind it. You will find inspiration as far as you are patient, penetrating what is hidden behind this word and its deep meaning.

- Even the objections that you find absurd may contain a lot of inspiration. Such objections will motivate you to find alternatives to solutions that you see as logical and thus will open your horizons to limitless possibilities.

- Sometimes you may have to say *no* when *yes* is the most logical response. Then, you need a lot of inspiration to justify your rejection.

- In general, there is no fear of rejection itself with regard to inspiration, unless you are rejecting appreciating the value of the inspiration itself.

- More than *no* and *not*, inspiration seems to be more closely related to *why not?*

- Rejection does not destroy inspiration itself; rather, it targets resolve. Make your resolve strong so that you will not lose the blessings of inspiration under any circumstances.

CREATIVITY AND INSPIRATION

10

- ☀ There is no creativity without inspiration. Inspiration is the fuel for creativity.

- ☀ Just as the forms of original creativity are not the same, every genuine creator deals with inspiration in their own way.

- ☀ Inspiration can be seen as the raw material, while creativity is the formation of that raw material.

- ☀ None of us lives without dealing with inspiration in some way, but creative persons owe a debt to inspiration more than others because their working lives essentially are based on it.

- ☀ The professional creative person does not circumvent inspiration itself but rather the methods of provoking it.

- ☀ Despite the creator's appreciation and gratitude for inspiration, the creator's relationship with inspiration constantly changes, given the nature of the inspiration in terms of the difficulty or smoothness of the flow and submission to the creator every time.

☼ When you find that inspiration is smoother and flows faster in a specific field but is more difficult in another, do not rush to judge the nature of inspiration in the field that you find difficult. Inspiration becomes smoother when you approach any field with interest, diligence, and deep passion.

☼ A person who is creative in more than one field does not necessarily have the same talent in every field. It is unwise, then, to expect to receive inspiration in every field in the same way.

☼ Those who study inspiration in detail are interested in the subject for academic purposes or out of curiosity. Creators automatically receive inspiration and develop themselves in it with focus and experience. It would be a good idea, however, for creators to study about inspiration in some detail, at least for a while. That will revive them in one way or another.

☼ The most sublime form of creativity is that through which deadlocks are broken, completely new springs are created, and previously unknown horizons are opened. While you are involved in your creative work, do not place restrictions on inspiration as it tries to find its way to you. Don't be intimidated by an idea, no matter how strange it may seem. You are creative as you are supposed to go out of the ordinary.

OBSTACLES TO INSPIRATION

- ⚯ Watch out for the glut. It is not important that you reach the point of saturation in understanding that by which you like to be inspired. On the contrary, you should leave yourself space to think and feel how to benefit from what you have absorbed.

- ⚯ Believe in inspiration with complete confidence, and you will get it. The greatest obstacle to inspiration, as in every concept in existence, is hesitating to believe in it so that each time you wait for the outcome to judge it.

- ⚯ Inspiration does not set a deadline. Don't be alarmed if inspiration slows down. Rest assured that the longer it takes to get to you, the more of it will come—so impulsive that it makes up for the delay.

- ⚯ It's hard to counter the intransigence of inspiration in relation to a particular idea in your head that you want to present to others. But getting annoyed and upset won't do you any good; on the contrary, that will have negative results. These negative results will affect not only the smoothness of the inspiration itself but your balance as well, with yourself and in front of others.

- ☼ Sometimes you may need a break to recharge before continuing inspirational work. Don't give in if you don't feel encouraged to go back to work. No matter how difficult it is to start again, don't hesitate to get back to work. Like most actions, inspiration sometimes needs a push in the beginning before it can resume at full speed.

- ☼ Don't let other people's disappointing comments affect your appreciation of the value of inspiration. Your deep confidence in your inspiring work and your patience with it until its impressive results are clear will ensure the recognition of others eventually.

- ☼ An obsession with following others and imitating them is one of the greatest obstacles to inspiration.

- ☼ Your preference for a certain routine in your daily life should not get in the way of inspiration in your work life. It is wise to break the routine, however, with some change from time to time; this will allow inspiration to bring a refreshing renewal into your daily lifestyle.

:ᄋ̣- Meditation is an action practiced in seclusion. Inspiration is a continuous state that should not be stopped, whether you are alone or with others.

:ᄋ̣- An intense fear of not meeting the expectations of others and breaking the norm will not necessarily hinder inspiration, but it certainly limits its flow and confines it in certain directions.

LEARNING AND TEACHING INSPIRATION

12

- ☼ Inspiration often comes suddenly, but that does not mean people should sit with folded hands, waiting for inspiration to fall on them from the sky. Deep thinking and reflection are the first steps in learning how to invoke inspiration.

- ☼ Inspiration becomes smoother through training and practice, but it never yields to the complete control of the creators, no matter how talented, skillful, or experienced they are.

- ☼ When you teach a few techniques for invoking inspiration, it may help people for a limited time, fleetingly. Make sure that you convey your own experiences—not what you have read—of inspiration to others with sincerity and love so that the inspiration becomes an experience for them that will last forever.

- ☼ While teaching or talking about inspiration with any group, do not hesitate to transfer your experience to the audience, regardless of their ages and categories. Inspiration does not recognize age or class. Focus on delivery rather than on content that is often accessible to everyone.

- ☼ In inspiration training, it is important that the mentor does not let the students' topic of interest distract him or her from opening the students' horizons to inspiration. The mentor should use inspiration's provoking experiences at all possible levels.

- ☼ The concept of leading by example is the basis of inspiration training. It is difficult to influence trainees if they do not feel that inspiration is continuously manifested in the mentor's attitude.

- ☼ Teaching inspiration does not mean offering a course with a few practical exercises and an exam at the end of the course. The main purpose of inspiration training is not for students to excel in the course or to complete a specific practical task successfully; rather, they should remain inspired continuously in their lives. However, the inspiration training sessions must be a continuous state of embodying the inspiration by the trainer and the trainees.

- ☼ The ingenuity of teaching inspiration is manifested in the trainer's skill in guiding their students to the most appropriate models of inspiration for each of them, specifically.

- ☀ Rather than teaching inspiration, work on inspiring inspiration.

- ☀ Life is the first teacher of inspiration, for which we do not directly pay. Look around you wherever you are, and you will find an inspiration source. All you need to take advantage of that source is deliberation and a deep desire for inspiration.

INSPIRATION AND AGE

13

- ☀ Inspiration is not directly related to age, but the inclinations of each individual certainly is. Inclinations and attitude change, according to one's age, and the expression of inspiring ideas and visions changes accordingly.

- ☀ It is necessary to be flexible to the changes that may occur in inspiration so that one can continue to benefit from the inspiration during various times of one's life. Inspiration is influenced by many factors throughout anyone's life, and age is one of these factors. But the effect of different age stages deserves special attention with regard to inspiration, as is the case with the effect of these stages on one's personal life at any level.

- ☀ All body parts age in terms of the ability to carry out their functions; the work that a person performs on every level decreases, in general. Inspiration itself does not seem to diminish with old age, but with old age, a person becomes less able and has less energy to accomplish inspiring works.

- Reflection increases and deepens with old age, so that deep reflection seems as if it were another form of inspiration in old age.

- Spontaneous and deep reflection on everything in life almost becomes the equivalent of inspiration in old age, even if that reflection does not lead to the achievement of new concrete actions, other than inspiring others to face and overcome life's difficulties.

- As you age, do not rush to attribute any problem with inspiration to aging. With the passage of time, many factors interfere in the life around you and affect you. Do not try to relieve yourself of the effort of working and thinking at relevant levels by blaming a lack of inspiration on growing old.

- Growing old gives you more experience and confidence, but it is important to be aware that this may lead to repetition in dealing with inspiration. Inspiration is essentially about innovation, and it is not possible to consider a repetitive idea an innovation that owes credit to any form of original inspiration.

- When you find inspiration pouring into you abundantly at a certain stage of life, do not waste your time wondering about the reasons and motives behind it. Make the best use of this opportunity and extract the maximum inspiration out of it.

- ☀ Do not postpone encountering inspiration difficulties and working on enhancing your approaches in dealing with inspiration for a future stage. You never know—maybe tomorrow's challenges will be more difficult. Strive to immediately overcome what hinders your dealing better with inspiration, and develop your skills in this significant aspect.

- ☀ The age at which the peak of inspiration is achieved varies greatly from person to person. Do not concern yourself with useless comparisons to others in this regard.

- ☀ The value of inspiration has nothing to do with a person's age. Do not hesitate to draw inspiration from the experiences of those who are younger than you with the same confidence and enthusiasm that you received inspiration from those who are older.

- ☀ The inspiration you received in your childhood generally stays with you for a lifetime. As it is said about learning, inspiration in childhood is like engraving in stone.

Receiving inspiration will not stop, but when you reach old age, you likely will inspire others more than you will receive inspiration from them.

INSPIRATION AND CULTURE

14

- People's appreciation of inspiration varies widely across cultures, from place to place, and from time to time. There is no nation or group of people that does not appreciate inspiration, but the themes and aspects of that appreciation often differ greatly.

- The difference in cultures in evaluating and valuing inspiration is not only among countries and large groups of people but also among families and even individuals within the same family.

- Creativity and innovation are, in fact, a reflection of how much inspiration is valued, whether for nations, groups, or individuals. Where creativity and innovation are abundant, there is a high value of inspiration within that culture.

- Inspiration usually does not seek permission from anyone, but the more open and daring the culture of individuals and their communities, the more daring the inspiration that the individuals receive. Daring inspiration probably knocks on everyone's door, but the self-censorship of conservative individuals causes them to not open their doors when those knocks of inspiration come—or even not to notice them at all.

☼ Getting to know a new culture increases and improves your reception of inspiration in general, as much as you are open to and assimilate to the new culture. When you deeply understand how others frame their culture and deal with it, that will not only affect your reception of inspiration for a time through a few examples inspired by the new culture, but also will reflect the impact of that culture on your inspiration in the long run.

☼ Every culture has known inspiration since ancient times, but no matter how advanced civilizations and their inventions and innovations are, every culture has its limitations and moral restrictions that impact the flow of inspiration in the nation's veins.

☼ There is no doubt that primitive human and ancient civilizations were more certain and faithful in dealing with inspiration that was directly related to nature. Nature was almost everything for them.

☼ Primitive humans, who had no other alternatives, believed in the power of inspiration from nature, and nature gave them what they needed. We now think that we have many alternatives, while all our inventions and innovations are directly or indirectly inspired by nature.

☀ Learning to deal with inspiration across civilizations and cultures is never one way. There is always something in any culture that can inspire others.

☀ The transferability of manifestations of inspiration is faster and smoother between close cultures. The deeper values that motivate the inspiration, however, are supposed to be exchanged between cultures that are more distant, as they include the newest and perhaps most strange sources of knowledge for each other.

INSPIRATION AS TREATMENT

15

- ☼ Before being considered as a treatment, inspiration is best viewed as prevention that is better than a cure, provided that people continue to approach it with deep interest in the various aspects of their lives.

- ☼ Inspiration does not necessarily constitute a direct treatment, but in most cases, inspiration works indirectly by guiding one to the most appropriate treatment and the best way to benefit from it.

- ☼ Inspiration works as a semi direct treatment when it provides deeply moving examples to others who have experienced difficult illness or adversity and who have overcome it with exciting success.

- ☼ One of the most important notes in the prescription for treatment with inspiration is to deeply believe in its effectiveness.

- We practice healing through inspiration when we ask those who have gone through the same experience about the treatment that has benefited them. But inspiration, in this case, does not mean being satisfied with the personal experiences of others, while not taking reliable medical treatment that is available, no matter how much time and effort it takes.

- Even direct medical treatment requires belief in its effectiveness in order to produce the desired results.

- Inspiration is a continuous cure for the soul's pains that does not disappoint those who resort to it. It must be remembered, however, that inspiration is not a magic wand that guarantees a miracle. Inspiration has long-lasting effects, but it often is not fast-acting.

- Patience and certitude seem to be the most important qualities that inspiration needs to achieve its desired benefits, not only with regard to treatment but on every level.

- Whatever their scientific skill and training, inspiration leads inspired therapists to reach the exact treatments of the cases presented faster than other therapists, who do not realize the importance of inspiration and deal with each case with a purely practical and methodological approach.

-ଡ଼- The importance of inspiration as a treatment is not only related to those who need therapy but also includes those who create and provide cures to others. Inspiration constitutes a main source of success with regard to reaching a new treatment, as well as determining the most appropriate scenario for dealing with each case among the available treatments.

INSPIRATION VALIDITY DATE

16

- ☼ Although it is tempting to view inspiration, in general, as having no expiration date, it is more accurate that the validity of benefiting from any inspiration experience depends on each case in terms of its originality, nature, and depth of impact on others.

- ☼ Any experience with inspiration, no matter how temporary or fleeting, does not exclude the possibility of benefiting from it in other experiences that are not necessarily identical or even similar to it.

- ☼ Just as the validity of inspiration is not related to a limited time in most cases, the inspiration—in terms of its validity in influencing people—doesn't exclude anyone, other than those who primarily do not open their minds and souls to receiving inspiration.

- ☼ When you find it difficult to get inspired in a particular situation, after serious attempts to reflect on similar experiences, do not hesitate to approach somewhat different and older experiences for you or others in general. You may find inspiration in some of those old experiences, but the most important thing is that these experiences will probably refresh you and invigorate you, preparing you to receive inspiration from available sources that you may not have considered.

- Inspiration related to feelings and emotions is often more persistent than that related to ideas.

- The inspiration you remember not only stays in your mind as a memory but remains influential.

- Don't be preoccupied with the "validity date" of a specific case of inspiration. The inspiration writes its expiration date by itself. All you have to do is be flexible in receiving the inspiration and be keen on making the most of it for as long as you can.

- Inspiration associated with a particular person will continue not only with that person's maintaining the behavior that inspired you but also with the continuation of the significance of that behavior to you.

- Don't be alarmed when you see that one of your inspirations has expired. This is a healthy, natural, and even necessary process to refresh your mind and soul. Your insistence on clinging to a form of inspiration that seems expired stands in the way of another form of inspiration that is waiting for your proper attention so it can flow into your mind and soul.

☀ Inspiration that seems to have expired may come back later, even after a long time, to knock on your mind and soul in one way or another.

INSPIRATION AND THE IMPOSSIBLE

17

- ☼ There is no impossible inspiration. Inspiration exists to overcome the impossible.

- ☼ Inspiration helps you discover that the impossible is often an understanding imposed on you by a special personal circumstance that you can overcome. Motivation through inspiration occurs when you see others go beyond what you consider impossible.

- ☼ If you find it difficult to get rid of the illusion of the impossible, inspiration at least should make you work constantly to raise the ceiling of the possible.

- ☼ To circumvent the illusion of the impossible, let inspiration help you find alternatives to what you think is impossible.

- ☼ Let your past experiences of getting beyond what you viewed as impossible inspire you to move beyond what you still see as impossible.

- The impossible is only adept at obscuring the possible behind it. Let inspiration help you find the possible that hides behind the impossible.

- If you still see that there are impossibilities that cannot be overcome, try not to let that thinking hinder your path, both personally and professionally. Far from looking at the possibility of finding alternatives to these "impossibles", let the inspiration enrich your life in all other fields at all levels. Don't let one thing or a few things, whatever they are, stop you from moving forward and enjoying the big life.

- If you insist on believing in the hidden power of the impossible, why shouldn't you also believe in the hidden secret of the miracle? In fact, your evaluation of both the impossible and the miracle depends on special circumstances you might encounter in certain situations, so that both the impossible and the miracle become part of the normal when those circumstances are gone.

- The impossible achieved by the effect of a miracle with regard to feelings and emotions is no less than the impossible achieved by the effect of a miracle with respect to theoretical and practical ideas and insights.

☀ Overcoming the impossible is not only learned from those you see as surpassing you in ability or achievements. You also will find great inspiration in the stories of those who missed out on many of the possibilities and abilities that you possess—and that did not prevent them from achieving what seemed impossible.

HOW DOES INSPIRATION
CHANGE YOUR LIFE?

18

☼ A single inspirational experience may make a drastic change in your life, but your deep and unwavering belief in inspiration is what makes you more confident, calm, and rich in visions throughout your life.

☼ Every inspirational experience brings you something new in your life, even if on a simple level. Celebrate every inspiration experience in your own way and make it a catalyst for more inspiration.

☼ The effect of uninterrupted inspiration is great on every level, but eventually, the issue is not with setting records in the number of inspiration experiences. The most important thing is the continuity of inspiration so that every experience is influential within your life. Get the most out of each experience of inspiration before becoming preoccupied with seeking the next one.

- ☀ When an experience of inspiration brings a drastic change in your life, celebrate it deeply, but do not stop there; don't let it distract you from moving forward on the path of inspiration. No matter how great the experience, don't let one person or one event take over most of your life while you can draw further inspiration from potentially richer sources.

- ☀ Although the great change that inspiration can bring to your life may come as a precious gift without prior connotations, it is generally important to be aware of the exact change to which you aspire in life so that inspiration can help you better.

- ☀ Continuous renewal and revival are the most sustainable changes that inspiration can make in your life. This requires that you be in an uninterrupted relationship with inspiration and approach it with skill, love, and sincerity.

- ☀ The effect of inspiration may come directly, but inspiration may refer you indirectly to what helps you to achieve an effect to which you aspire—or even one that you did not think of. In all cases, treat signs of inspiration with fineness and care, and do not underestimate these signs, no matter how fleeting or worthless they may seem.

- One of the greatest influences of inspiration on your life is to remain a source of inspiration to others.

- The impact of inspiration becomes deeper in your life when you make sure that you inspire others and receive inspiration from them and from every possible source in life.

- It is good to celebrate the great change that inspiration has brought into your life on any level at any stage. But it is important to realize that life is constantly changing, so do not close the door to future changes that will follow. The effect of other experiences of inspiration may have results completely different from what you reached in your current experience, no matter how great and favorable the results of the current experience seem to you.

Printed in the United States
by Baker & Taylor Publisher Services